The NEW ABCs of

FINANCIAL FREEDOM
WORKBOOK

BARRY L. CAMERON

TABLE OF CONTENTS

MY NOTES

INTRODUCTION

Financial Freedom is within reach of every single individual, family, church and organization in the world. But it won't just happen. You have to be willing to make the effort necessary to reach your goals.

To get where you can finally declare your *Financial Freedom* will require the following:
   a. God's wisdom and applying His principles
   b. Time and patience
   c. Discipline and determination
   d. Persistence and consistency
   e. A clearly defined plan

For best results, this workbook should be used in a small group setting for accountability, encouragement, and motivation as you pursue Financial Freedom with others. Each week you will work through a specific study, have a time of interaction discussing God's principles, and then, have the opportunity to make personal application to your own situation.

Being part of a small group will help you achieve your financial goals. Research has repeatedly shown the value of working with others in the achieving of goals whether they are physical, relational, financial, professional, or spiritual. The Bible says, "*Two are better than one, because they have a good return for their work: If one falls down, his friend can help him up*" **(Ecclesiastes 4:9-10a)**.

This workbook is simple and practical so anyone, regardless of age or financial status, can easily understand and apply God's principles and achieve *Financial Freedom*. It was designed as a companion to *The ABCs of Financial Freedom*. If you haven't read the book, you will need to do so before beginning.

REMEMBER
You can't claim God's promises if you don't follow His principles. But if you do ...
... you will achieve *Financial Freedom!*

Barry L. Cameron, Senior Pastor
Crossroads Christian Church
Grand Prairie, Texas

"*The blessing of the Lord brings wealth, and he adds no trouble to it*" **(Proverbs 10:22)**.

MY SMALL GROUP MEMBERS

NAME	PHONE	EMAIL
1.		
2.		
3.		
4.		
5.		
6.		
7.		
8.		
9.		
10.		
11.		
12.		
13.		
14.		
15.		

MY SMALL GROUP COMMITMENT

It's a great idea for every small group to have an understanding of the expectations before you begin. In order to help your group, we have listed a number of items below for you to talk about and agree upon before you begin.

We agree to the following VALUES:

1. Our small group exists to honor the Lord, encourage one another and hold each other accountable.

2. Attending our small group meeting each week is a priority to us. (I will call if I have to be absent or late.)

3. We will keep everything shared in our small group strictly confidential. We want our group to be a safe place for people to share their heart and get the help they need.

4. We give other small group members permission to help us live a healthy, balanced, spiritual life that is pleasing to God.

5. We will invite our friends who would benefit from this study and will gladly welcome all newcomers.

6. We will pray regularly for one another.

7. We will care for and minister to each other beyond this study.

We have also discussed and agree upon the following items:

Childcare arrangements: _____

Where we will meet: _____

Starting time: _____ Ending time: _____

Signed: _____

Dated: _____

WEEK 1: ATTITUDE

Opening Prayer

Welcome: Take a few minutes to introduce yourself to each other.
"What is your favorite movie? Why? Who is someone you admire? Why?"

Scripture:
- Have someone read **Proverbs 17:16**.
- Have someone else read **Luke 16:10-12**.

What do these verses teach us about money?
Answer these three questions:

Why would God give us more money when we've been foolish with what He's already given us?

How can we get more of God's wisdom?

If we can't be trusted (or have been dishonest) with little, will God ever give us much?

If we want to achieve *Financial Freedom*, we'll have to change our attitude toward money and how we manage it.

John Maxwell said, "When our attitudes outdistance our abilities, even the impossible becomes possible." What seems impossible today can become possible if we are willing to change our attitude.

The reality is, the reason nothing changes in our lives is often because nothing changes. We keep doing the same thing year after year expecting things to get better – but they don't.

WHAT CHANGES WOULD YOU BE WILLING TO MAKE IN ORDER TO CHANGE YOUR FINANCIAL SITUATION?

Remember, nothing changes until something (or someone) changes.

The Cameron family had a number of "come to Jesus" meetings to decide changes they would make to get out of debt. Look at some of the things they did.

CHANGES THE CAMERON FAMILY MADE

1. We all went on strict budgets and there were no exceptions.
2. We cancelled our subscription to the local newspaper and to USA TODAY.
3. We cancelled all magazine subscriptions.
4. We cancelled cable TV.
5. We took sack lunches to school and work (all of us).
6. We didn't go out to eat.
7. We stopped getting our dog groomed.
8. We didn't go to movies.
9. We cut back on haircuts.
10. We didn't go to concerts.
11. We didn't do any special treatments for my wife or our girls - nails, perms, etc.
12. We didn't go to sporting events.
13. We didn't go anywhere you had to purchase a ticket.
14. We had our older kids get jobs.
15. We started drinking water instead of paying for coffee, tea or soft drinks.
16. We turned down a lot of invitations to do things in order to save money.
17. We went without new clothes for two years.
18. We didn't go on any vacations or trips for two years.
19. We carpooled to church to save on gas.
20. We had a garage sale.
21. We turned the thermostat up in the summer and down in the winter.
22. We turned lights off when we left a room.
23. We unplugged anything that blinked, buzzed, hummed, or gave any indication it was costing us money unless we were using it.
24. We consolidated all trips to conserve gas.
25. We stopped watering our grass. (Yes, our yard turned to dirt.)
26. We didn't leave the water running while we brushed our teeth.

27. We took less baths and shorter showers.

28. We used coupons when shopping for groceries and necessities.

29. We used birthday money, Christmas money, etc., to pay down the mortgage on our house.

30. We reduced what we normally spent on Christmas and only gave gifts to each other that were practical – things we needed.

31. We informed extended family members we wouldn't be exchanging gifts in order to help us get out of debt.

32. We didn't put Christmas lights on the outside of our house.

33. We didn't buy furniture.

34. We didn't buy DVDs or CDs.

35. We had our kids pay for their own stuff at school, camp, etc.

36. We developed a laser focus of paying off our debts, including our mortgage, and looked for every dime and dollar we could find to do so.

37. We used less of everything – shampoo, toothpaste, etc., so it would last longer.

CHANGES YOU CAN MAKE

Take a moment and check each box that represents something you would be willing to do in order to get out of debt. (Remember: Nothing changes if nothing changes.)

☐ 1. Go on a strict budget with no exceptions.

☐ 2. Cancel your subscription to the local newspaper.

☐ 3. Cancel all magazine subscriptions.

☐ 4. Cancel cable TV.

☐ 5. Take a sack lunch to school/work.

☐ 6. Don't go out to eat.

☐ 7. Stop getting pets groomed.

☐ 8. Don't go to movies.

☐ 9. Cut back on haircuts.

☐ 10. Don't go to concerts.

☐ 11. Don't do any special treatments like nails, perms, etc.

☐ 12. Don't go to sporting events.

☐ 13. Don't go to anything where you have to purchase a ticket.

☐ 14. Encourage your older children to get jobs.

☐ 15. Start drinking water instead of paying for coffee, tea or soft drinks.

☐ 16. Turn down invitations to do things in order to save money.

☐ 17. Go without new clothes until you are debt free.

☐ 18. Don't go on any vacations or trips until you are debt free.

☐ 19. Carpool to church to save on gas.

☐ 20. Have a garage sale.

☐ 21. Turn the thermostat up in the summer and down in the winter.

☐ 22. Turn lights off when you leave a room.

☐ 23. Unplug anything that blinks, buzzes, hums, or gives any indication it is costing money unless you are using it.

☐ 24. Consolidate all trips to conserve gas.

☐ 25. Stop watering the yard.

☐ 26. Don't leave the water running while brushing your teeth.

☐ 27. Take less baths and shorter showers.

☐ 28. Use coupons when shopping for groceries and necessities.

☐ 29. Use birthday money, Christmas money, etc., to pay down the mortgage on the house.

☐ 30. Reduce what you normally spend on Christmas and only give gifts to each other that are practical – things you need.

☐ 31. Inform extended family members you won't be exchanging gifts in order to help you get out of debt.

☐ 32. Don't put Christmas lights on the outside of your house at Christmas time.

☐ 33. Don't buy furniture.

☐ 34. Don't buy DVDs or CDs.

☐ 35. Have children pay for their own stuff at school, camp, etc.

☐ 36. Develop a laser focus of paying off all debts, including the mortgage.

☐ 37. Use less of everything – shampoo, toothpaste, etc., so it will last longer.

CHANGE BEGINS WITH OUR ATTITUDE

Here's how we can begin to change our attitude:

1. **Acknowledge the sovereignty of God in our finances.**

    Psalm 24:1 says, "The earth is the Lord's and everything in it, the world and all who live in it."

    Simply put, everything belongs to God. We are just managers of whatever He gives us.

    It's foolish to think what we have is really ours.

    That's the essence of the parable Jesus told in **Luke 12:16-20**.

    Jesus told them this parable: "*The ground of a certain rich man produced a good crop. He thought to himself, 'What shall I do? I have no place to store my crops.'*

    "*Then he said, 'This is what I'll do. I will tear down my barns and build bigger ones, and there I will store all my grain and my goods. And I'll say to myself, "You have plenty of good things laid up for many years. Take life easy; eat, drink and be merry."'*

    "*But God said to him, 'You fool! This very night your life will be demanded from you. Then who will get what you have prepared for yourself?'*"

2. **Recognize whatever we have is on temporary loan from God.**

    Job said, "*Naked I came from my mother's womb, and naked I will depart*" **(Job 1:21)**.

    Whatever God gives us is only for a little while. Our responsibility is to be faithful managers of whatever He gives us. **(See 1 Corinthians 4:2; Matthew 25:14-30.)**

3. **Realize we can change our financial situation if we will get more of God's wisdom and apply His principles to our finances.**

    Matthew 6:33, "*But seek first His (God's) Kingdom and His righteousness, and all these things will be given to you as well.*"

    Deuteronomy 8:18, "*But remember the Lord your God, for it is He who gives you the ability to produce wealth, and so confirms His covenant, which he swore to your forefathers, as it is today.*"

HOMEWORK

1. List three additional ideas, besides what's on the Cameron's list, that you could do to get out of debt.

#1 – _____

#2 – _____

#3 – _____

2. Pray for the other members of your group and their financial situation.

3. Invite a friend who could use this study to come with you next week.

4. Read through next week's lesson and fill in the blanks.

WEEK 2: BONDAGE

Opening Prayer

Welcome: Go around the room and have each group member answer one of these questions.

> *"When you were a child, what did you want to be when you grew up?" "If you had a day all to yourself, what would you do?"*

Scripture:
- Have someone read Proverbs 22:7.
- Have someone else read Romans 13:8.

What do these verses teach us about debt?

1. Debt makes us a _____ to someone other than God.

2. The only debt we should have is to _____ one another.

The first step on the road to *Financial Freedom* is to **acknowledge the sovereignty of God in our finances.**

a. It all belongs to Him **(Psalm 24:1)**.
b. It all comes from Him **(Deuteronomy 8:18; 1 Chronicles 29:10-14)**.
c. We are simply managers for Him **(1 Corinthians 4:2; Matthew 25:14-30)**.

The second step on the road to *Financial Freedom* is to **be aware of and avoid the subtlety of debt.**

Financial expert, David Bach, says, "The reality of life is that just about everyone in America makes enough money to be wealthy. So why aren't we all rich? The problem isn't our income, it's what we spend." (*Smart Couples Finish Rich*)

The truth about debt is: With the exception of purchasing a home, when you go into debt for something, that thing begins to depreciate in value the moment you buy it.

READ AND DISCUSS THESE SEVEN BIBLICAL PRINCIPLES CONCERNING DEBT:

1. Going into debt makes you a servant to someone other than God.

   Proverbs 22:7, *"The rich rule over the poor, and the borrower is servant to the lender."*

2. It's clearly a sin if you borrow and don't repay.

   Psalm 37:21, *"The wicked borrow and do not repay, but the righteous give generously."*

3. The Bible warns that it is better not to go into debt.

   Proverbs 17:18, *"A man lacking in judgment strikes hands in pledge and puts up security for his neighbor."*

4. The longest term of debt God's people took on in the Bible was seven years.

   Deuteronomy 15:1, *"At the end of every seven years you must cancel debts."*

5. You are not in control of your future.

   James 4:13-15, *"Now, listen, you who say, 'Today or tomorrow we will go to this or that city, spend a year there, carry on business and make money.' Why, you do not even know what will happen tomorrow. What is your life? You are a mist that appears for a little while and then vanishes. Instead, you ought to say, 'If it is the Lord's will, we will live and do this or that.'"*

6. When you go into debt, you are asking someone other than God to meet your needs.

   Philippians 4:19, *"And my God will meet all your needs according to his glorious riches in Christ Jesus."*

7. When you go into debt and mortgage your future, you affect your whole family.

   Proverbs 11:28-29, *"Whoever trusts in his riches will fall, but the righteous will thrive like a green leaf. He who brings trouble on his family will inherit only wind, and the fool will be servant to the wise."*

What do you think God is trying to tell you concerning debt? (Check one)

☐ Take on more debt   ☐ Get out of debt

☐ Don't sweat your debt   ☐ Don't change anything

Most people have no idea the load they are unnecessarily carrying because of their debt. Here's an example of how to determine the **L.O.A.D.** you are carrying:

LISTING OF ALL DEBTS

CREDITOR	PURCHASE	MONTHLY PAYMENT	BALANCE OWED	INTEREST RATE
First National	Home	$ 930	$102,000	4.5%
GMAC	Car	$ 425	$ 26,000	6%
TMC	Car	$ 365	$ 14,500	5%
Master Card	Misc.	$ 40	$ 3,800	17%
Visa	Misc.	$ 35	$ 4,100	18%
Credit Union	School loan	$ 150	$ 15,000	5%
TOTALS		**$1,945.00**	**$165,400.00**	

HOMEWORK

1. Determine the L.O.A.D. you are carrying by listing all your debts on the worksheet provided.

2. Make the irrevocable commitment to God and to yourself that you are going to get out of debt.

3. Pray for the other members of your group and their financial situation.

4. Invite a friend who could use this study to come with you next week.

5. Read through next week's lesson, and fill in the blanks.

LISTING OF ALL DEBTS

CREDITOR	PURCHASE	MONTHLY PAYMENT	BALANCE OWED	INTEREST RATE
TOTALS				

WEEK 3: CHOICE

Opening Prayer

Welcome: Go around the room and have each group member answer this question.
"Where is your favorite place to go on vacation and why?"

We have the power to choose …
Life affords us all kinds of choices. Where to live, where to work, who to marry, where we go on vacation, etc. But the greatest choice we ever make is when we choose to obey God and do things His way.

Scripture:

- **Read 1 Samuel 15:22** and fill in the blanks below.

  "To _____ is better than _____."

- **Read Proverbs 3:9-10** and fill in the blanks below.

  "Honor the Lord with your _____, with the _____ of all your crops. Then your barns will be _____ to overflowing, and your vats will brim over with new wine."

- **Read Matthew 6:33** and fill in the blanks below.

  "But seek _____ His (God's) kingdom and His righteousness, and all these _____ will be _____ to you as well."

The first two steps on the road to *Financial Freedom* are:
1. **Acknowledge the sovereignty of God in our finances.**
2. **Be aware of and avoid the subtlety of debt.**

The third step on the road to *Financial Freedom* is:
3. **Obey God and adopt the centrality of the tithe in your financial plans. In other words, make tithing the centerpiece of your personal financial plan.**

WHAT IS THE TITHE?

The tithe is 10 percent of our income, which we give to God every week.
Malachi 3:10-12 says,

> "'*Bring the whole tithe into the storehouse (the local church), that there may be food in my house. Test me in this,' says the Lord Almighty, 'and see if I will not throw open the floodgates of Heaven and pour out so much blessing that you will not have room enough for it. I will prevent pests from devouring your crops, and the vines in your fields will not cast their fruit,' says the Lord Almighty. 'Then all the nations will call you blessed, for yours will be a delightful land,' says the Lord Almighty.*"

Tithing is a timeless principle, instituted by God to bless His people. It's not a **money** issue. It's a **master** issue. Who is our master? Money or God? Jesus said we can't serve both. We have to choose.

> "No one can serve two masters. He will hate the one and love the other, or he will be devoted to the one and despise the other. You cannot serve both God and Money" **(Matthew 6:24)**.

According to **Leviticus 27:30,** who does the tithe belong to? _____

Read **Malachi 3:10-12** (above) again. Do you realize God makes a distinct and absolutely unique promise in those verses that is not repeated anywhere else in the Bible? God promises to "throw open the floodgates of Heaven and pour out so much blessing that you will not have enough room for it."

If we do what? Pray? Read the Bible? Share our faith? Help the poor? No. Even though we should do all of that. None of those things will cause God to "throw open the floodgates of Heaven" and bless us with so much we "will not have room enough for it."

There is only **ONE THING** God says we can do, that when we do it He promises to "throw open the floodgates of Heaven and pour out so much blessing that you will not have room enough for it." He even says to **TEST HIM** in this.

What does God say is that ONE THING? _____

Tithing is **elementary**. It's an entry point for believers, not an ending point; it's a beginning point. Tithing is how we "get under the spout where God's blessings come out."

LET'S REVIEW

1. We have the power to _____.

2. Tithing is not a MONEY issue, it's a _____ issue.

3. The tithe belongs to _____, not us.

4. We are to bring the "whole tithe" into the storehouse (the local church).

5. _____ is how we get "under the spout where God's blessings come out."

WHEN IT COMES TO TITHING, WHAT DOES GOD SAY WE ARE TO DO?
(Check the appropriate box.)

☐ Pray about it.

☐ Pay all your bills first and, if there is any money left over, give whatever you can.

☐ Bring the whole tithe into His storehouse (the local church).

☐ Ask your friends to tithe for you.

HOW MUCH IS A TITHE? (Check the appropriate box.)

☐ 2 percent

☐ 5 percent

☐ Whatever you decide you want to give

☐ 10 percent

☐ 15 percent

HOMEWORK

1. **Choose to obey God and begin tithing this week.**

2. **Develop a budget - G.O.O.D. file (Get Out Of Debt).** An example is provided on the following worksheet where you can fill in your personal amounts and get a picture of your finances each month.

3. **Pray for the other members of your group and their financial situation.**

4. **Invite a friend to join your group next week.**

5. **Read through next week's lesson, and fill in the blanks.**

G.O.O.D. FILE (Budget)

Monthly Salary:	_____	Restaurants:	_____
Other Income:	_____	Movies/Concerts:	_____
Total Income:	_____	Babysitter:	_____
Subtract:		Vacation:	_____
Tithe:	_____	Other:	_____
Taxes:	_____	**Total Entertainment Expenses:**	_____
Monthly Spendable Income:	_____	**Clothing:**	_____
Mortgage/Rent:	_____	Dentist:	_____
Insurance:	_____	Doctor:	_____
Taxes:	_____	Prescriptions:	_____
Electric:	_____	**Total Medical Payments:**	_____
Gas:	_____	**Savings:**	_____
Water:	_____		
Satellite/Cable:	_____	Child care/school:	_____
Phone/Internet:	_____	Cell phone:	_____
Maintenance:	_____	Haircuts/nails:	_____
Other:	_____	Dry cleaning:	_____
Total Housing Expenses:	_____	Lunches:	_____
Groceries:	_____	Toiletries:	_____
		Subscriptions:	_____
Auto Payments:	_____	Allowance/cash:	_____
Gas:	_____	Holiday/Birthday Gifts:	_____
Auto Insurance:	_____	**Total Personal Expenses:**	_____
Other:	_____		
Total Auto Expenses:	_____		
		Total Expenses:	_____
Medical:	_____		
Life:	_____	**Monthly Spendable Income:**	_____
Health:	_____	**Less Total Expenses:**	_____
Total Insurance Payments:	_____	**Surplus (Deficit):**	_____

Week 4: DECISION

Opening Prayer

Welcome: As you begin, ask group members to answer this question.
"What are the two best decisions you've ever made?"

Where we are today is the direct result of the decisions we made in the past. Where we will be tomorrow will be determined by the decisions we make today.

So far we've seen we need to:
1. **Acknowledge the sovereignty of God in our finances.**
2. **Be aware of and avoid the subtlety of debt.**
3. **Choose to make tithing the centerpiece of our financial plan.**

The next thing we need to do is:
4. **Decide to do things God's way in our finances and in every area of our lives.**

Scripture:

- **Read Proverbs 14:12** and fill in the blanks below.

   "There is a way that seems _____ to a man, but in the end it leads to _____."

- **Read Proverbs 3:5-6** and fill in the blanks below.

   "Trust in the _____ with all your heart and lean not on your _____ understanding; in all your ways acknowledge Him, and he will make your paths _____."

Doing what's right is never easy, nor does it usually happen overnight. There will be plenty of opposition (people who don't understand why you're doing what you're doing) and plenty of opportunities for you to rationalize not staying on track to reach your goals. There will be lots of challenges as you pursue your goal of *Financial Freedom*. But you can make it if you will stick by your decision to be debt free.

T. BOONE PICKENS once said,

"Be willing to make decisions. That's the most important quality in a good leader. Don't fall victim to what I call the 'ready-aim-aim-aim syndrome.' You must be willing to fire."

REVIEW THE SEVEN SIMPLE STRATEGIES TO GET OUT OF DEBT:

1. **Trust God (Matthew 6:33)**

   "But seek first His (God's) Kingdom and His righteousness, and all these things will be given to you as well."

   Make God the #1 pursuit of your life and everything else will take care of itself.

2. **Tithe (Malachi 3:10-12)**

   "'Bring the whole tithe into the storehouse (the local church), that there may be food in my house. Test me in this,' says the Lord Almighty, 'and see if I will not throw open the floodgates of Heaven and pour out so much blessing that you will not have room enough for it. I will prevent pests from devouring your crops, and the vines in your fields will not cast their fruit,' says the Lord Almighty. 'Then all the nations will call you blessed, for yours will be a delightful land,' says the Lord Almighty."

   Every weekend bring the tithe from your income that week and give it back to God as an act of obedience, trusting in Him for His provision and protection for your finances.

3. **Develop A Budget (Luke 14:28-29)**

   "Suppose one of you wants to build a tower. Will he not first sit down and estimate the cost to see if he has enough money to complete it? For if he lays the foundation and is not able to finish it, everyone who sees it will ridicule him."

   You need to have a budget **(Get Out Of Debt file)**. If you're married, both spouses need to see the whole picture of your finances on a regular basis.

4. **Get Out Of Debt (Proverbs 22:7)**

   "The rich rule over the poor, and the borrower is servant to the lender."

   The first step to getting out of debt is not to get into any more debt. Then, begin paying off the debts you already have.

   Remember the word INTEREST: If you're paying interest, someone else is getting wealthy, not you.

Remember what the letters D-E-B-T stand for: Don't Even Buy That! Or a Dumb Explanation for Buying Things.

5. Put Something In Savings Every Week (Proverbs 13:11)

"Dishonest money dwindles away, but he who gathers money little by little makes it grow."

Always spend less than you make each week and always put something in savings.

Each week, after you give God the tithe, try to save 10 percent.

6. Develop An Emergency Fund (Proverbs 6:6-11)

"Go to the ant, you sluggard; consider its ways and be wise! It has no commander, no overseer or ruler, yet it stores its provisions in summer and gathers its food at harvest. How long will you lie there, you sluggard? When will you get up from your sleep? A little sleep, a little slumber, a little folding of the hands to rest – and poverty will come on you like a bandit and scarcity like an armed man."

Plan for a rainy day, because it will rain. Don't use your emergency fund for dinner, a concert, vacation, etc. Save it for emergencies and let it grow.

You need to have a will.

7. Don't Quit Or Turn Back (Luke 9:62)

"Jesus replied, 'No one who puts his hand to the plow and looks back is fit for service in the Kingdom of God.'"

To see how you're doing, complete the *Financial Freedom* checklist below. (Check the boxes that pertain to you.)

I have...
- ☐ Made the decision to get out of debt
- ☐ Made a list of changes to help me get out of debt
- ☐ Made a list of all current debts (see **L.O.A.D.** chart)
- ☐ Made a budget (**G.O.O.D.** file) and have begun to follow it
- ☐ Made tithing the centerpiece of my financial plan

HOMEWORK

1. **Complete the rapid payoff strategy for your debts (see following page).**
    You should list each debt, on the worksheet provided, beginning with the smallest at the top to the largest at the bottom. Total the amount, then, begin paying them off in descending order. Once you eliminate a debt, use the funds from that previous payment to double up on your next one. You'll be surprised how quickly this works.

2. **Pray for the rest of the members in your group regarding their finances.**

3. **Invite a friend to join your group next week.**

4. **Read through next week's lesson, and fill in the blanks.**

RAPID PAYOFF STRATEGY FOR YOUR DEBTS

CREDITOR	CONTACT NUMBER	PAYOFF AMOUNT	MONTHLY PAYMENT	INTEREST RATE
Shell	888.555.5551	$ 165.00	$ 20.00	19%
JC Penney	888.555.5552	$ 330.00	$ 25.00	21%
Sears	888.555.5553	$ 410.00	$ 35.00	22%
Target	888.555.5554	$ 530.00	$ 40.00	20%
MasterCard	888.555.5555	$ 1,100.00	$ 30.00	15%
Visa	888.555.5556	$ 5,200.00	$ 90.00	18%
Roomstore	888.555.5557	$ 6,500.00	$ 125.00	7%
University Credit	888.555.5558	$ 14,200.00	$ 140.00	6%
GMAC	888.555.5559	$ 18,500.00	$ 445.00	6%
First National	888.555.5550	$162,000.00	$1,650.00	4.5%
TOTAL		$208,935.00	$2,600.00	

RAPID PAYOFF STRATEGY FOR YOUR DEBTS

CREDITOR	CONTACT NUMBER	PAYOFF AMOUNT	MONTHLY PAYMENT	INTEREST RATE
TOTAL				

WEEK 5: ENCOURAGEMENT

Opening Prayer

Welcome: Have the members of your group answer this question:

"What's the most unique thing you've ever done to encourage someone else?"

Scripture:

- **Read Romans 12:6-8.**

  In verse 8, Paul lists _____ as one of the gifts God has given to the body of Christ.

- **Read 1 Thessalonians 5:11** and fill in the blanks below.

  We are to "_____ one another and _____ each other up, just as in fact you are doing."

Hopefully, you've already been encouraged and built up by being a part of this study.

If you have …

- **Acknowledged the sovereignty of God in your finances**
- **Become aware of and decided to avoid the subtlety of debt**
- **Chosen to make tithing the centerpiece of your financial plan**
- **Decided to do things God's way in your finances and in every area of your life**

… you should be encouraged.

A POWERFUL TESTIMONY

C.J. Teubert of Huntington, West Virginia, never made more than $6,000 a year during his career as a postal worker, and he used to wear secondhand clothes. His last will and testament was scribbled on the back of an old business letter. However, when he died at the age of 91, he left an estate worth more than $3 million, most of which he left to helping the American Foundation for the Blind, headquartered in New York. His gift will keep on giving forever.

Does that encourage you? It should.

Here's the point: It's not how much you make that will determine your ultimate wealth. Rather, it will be what you do with what you already have.

How long does it take to reach *Financial Freedom*?

Have you ever noticed the phenomenon that happens with the gas gauge in your automobile?

When you first fill up with gas, it seems as if the needle takes forever to move from FULL to HALF.

But, once you get to the halfway mark, it seems to fall to EMPTY much quicker.

Ever notice that?

Why do you think that is? No one knows for sure.

The same thing will happen with your finances. It may seem like it takes forever to reduce your debt and to increase your savings.

It may seem like you're not making any progress at all.

Just keep doing what you're supposed to be doing and watch what happens. In time, just like your gas gauge, your debt will fall and your savings will rise.

It won't happen overnight, and it won't happen without effort on your part.

You should have already completed the following:
1. Made tithing the centerpiece of your financial plan.
2. Made a list of the things you can change to start getting out of debt.
3. Made a list of all of your debts so you know the load you're carrying.
4. Developed a budget (your **G.O.O.D.** file) so you know how much you have coming in and how much is going out each month.
5. Completed the Rapid Debt Payoff Strategy sheet to eliminate your debts, listing each amount owed from the smallest to the largest.

A THREE-PART STRATEGY THAT WORKS!
In order to achieve *Financial Freedom*, there are three essential things you must do:

1. **Tithe.** You need God's wisdom, provision and protection to turn your financial situation around.

2. **Save.** You need to be putting something in savings every week, even if it seems like a minimal amount to you.

3. **Pay down your debt.** You need to apply every additional dollar you can find to pay off your debts.

THE POWER OF THE TITHE
Why does tithing work?

Read Deuteronomy 8:18 and fill in the blank below.

"But remember the Lord your God, for it is _____ who gives you the ability to produce wealth, and so confirms His covenant."

• God is the One Who gives us the ability to produce wealth.

Read Malachi 3:10 and fill in the blank below.

"Bring the whole tithe into the storehouse (the local church), that there may be food in my house. Test me in this," says the Lord Almighty, "and see if _____ will not throw open the floodgates of Heaven and pour out so much blessing that you will not have room enough for it."

• God is the One Who promises to provide for us. He is the One Who throws open the floodgates of Heaven and pours out so much blessing we won't have room for it all.

According to **Malachi 3:10**, what triggers the floodgates of Heaven to open upon us?

_____

CHRISTIAN FINANCIAL EXPERT LARRY BURKETT SAID:

"The word tithe literally means a tenth. Since this is the minimum amount mentioned in the Bible, it would be logical to assume that it's the minimum amount God wants from a believer. If we can't return even the smallest part to God, it merely testifies that the whole has never been surrendered to Him. In the book of Malachi, the prophet confronted God's people with the fact that they didn't love Him. Yet, they said that they did love Him. But the evidence against them was that they didn't give. This is the only place in Scripture where God ever told His people to test Him. Plus this passage makes the principle of tithing clear. It's an outside indicator of an inside spiritual condition. It's our testimony that God owns everything." **(Larry Burkett, *Answers To Your Family's Financial Questions*)**

THE POWER OF SAVING

Why does something as simple as saving a little each week make such a big difference?

Read Proverbs 13:11 and fill in the blank below.

"Dishonest money dwindles away, but he who gathers money little by little, makes it _____."

If you could find a way to save ...

- $5 a week   x   52 weeks   = $260
- $10 a week   x   52 weeks   = $520
- $15 a week   x   52 weeks   = $780
- $20 a week   x   52 weeks   = $1,040
- $25 a week   x   52 weeks   = $1,300
- $30 a week   x   52 weeks   = $1,560

Over a period of five years that would amount to ...

- $5 a week   x   5 years   = $1,300
- $10 a week   x   5 years   = $2,600
- $15 a week   x   5 years   = $3,900
- $20 a week   x   5 years   = $5,200
- $25 a week   x   5 years   = $6,500
- $30 a week   x   5 years   = $7,800

Now, let's stretch a bit. What if you could find a way to save ...

- $50 a week   x   52 weeks   = $2,600
- $60 a week   x   52 weeks   = $3,120
- $75 a week   x   52 weeks   = $3,900
- $80 a week   x   52 weeks   = $4,160
- $90 a week   x   52 weeks   = $4,680
- $100 a week   x   52 weeks   = $5,200

Over a period of five years that would amount to ...

- $ 50 a week   x   5 years   = $13,000
- $ 60 a week   x   5 years   = $15,600
- $ 75 a week   x   5 years   = $19,500
- $ 80 a week   x   5 years   = $20,800
- $ 90 a week   x   5 years   = $23,400
- $100 a week   x   5 years   = $26,000

- The discipline of saving something each week will produce tremendous results. But where can you find the extra money to do it?
    - A large drink at Sonic
    - A Starbucks White Chocolate Peppermint Mocha
    - US Weekly magazine
    - A pint of Ben & Jerry's
    - iTunes downloads
    - DVDs

Take a moment and discuss where you might find extra money to save.

ADDITIONAL SOURCES WHERE YOU CAN FIND MONEY TO SAVE:

1. Pray and ask God for His supernatural provision as you trust Him to provide for you.

2. Do some plastic surgery. Cut up some of your credit cards.

3. Call or meet with your insurance agent annually to consider the possible benefits of raising deductibles on your auto, home, and health insurance. Make sure you have money in savings or your emergency fund to cover any additional potential cost.

4. Check to see if you have PMI (mortgage insurance) on your house payment. Some mortgage companies don't require it once your mortgage has been paid down to a certain point. (It's worth checking out.)

5. Check with your cell phone company to have certain services removed that you don't really need.

6. Check with your provider to see if a bundle (TV + internet + phone) is available at a reduced cost.

7. Ask the police to do a home safety inspection. Many home insurance companies offer a discount if you have the inspection and/or purchase an alarm-monitoring service.

8. If you are a member of a professional association, see if a lifetime membership is less expensive than an annual fee.

9. Consider taking a break from memberships that require a fee, like a fitness club, golf club, etc., until you are out of debt.

10. Check with your auto insurance company to see if taking a defensive driving class would lower your coverage costs. You can take the class online.

11. To lower gas costs, check out the discount gasoline cards offered at places like Walmart/Sam's Club, RaceTrac, etc.

12. Compare switching to a lower cost term life insurance instead of whole life. Don't however, make any snap decisions without first seeking appropriate counsel.

13. Give yourself a pay raise. Check your W-4 form. Don't have your employer take out too much federal income tax during the year just so you can get a refund. That's not good stewardship.

14. Look into starting a part-time home business or partnering with a friend in house cleaning, lawn care, providing child care, putting up Christmas lights, etc., to supplement your income.

15. Move your thermostat two degrees per day from wherever you normally have it for as many days as you can. You won't notice the difference in your home, but you will notice a difference in your bill.

16. Turn off the TV. You will save energy, read more, have more time to spend with your family and save a few $$$ on your electric bill.

17. Be creative, like carpooling to work and co-oping with others for needs like child care.

18. Collect all your change in a jar and take it to your bank every two weeks or so. Most banks have machines that will count your change for free if you deposit money there.

19. Eliminate all snacks from your diet. You will save money, lose weight, feel and look better.

20. Plan your errands so you can reduce the number of trips you have to make each week.

21. Have a meeting with your family (if you are married/have kids) and ask everyone for their ideas on saving money.

22. To save money on food, become a coupon clipper. Check out thegrocerygame.com for more information.

THE POWER OF PAYING DOWN YOUR DEBTS
Read Proverbs 22:7 and fill in the blank below.

"The rich rule over the poor, and the borrower is _____ to the lender."

- Once you pay off your debts, you will no longer be anyone's servant other than God's!

- Imagine what you could do this week if your paycheck wasn't already precommitted to payments to some financial institution.

What would you do with your paycheck this week if you could do anything you want with it?

_____

• If you will discipline yourself, that can happen much quicker than you ever dreamed.

Proverbs 13:18 says, "He who ignores discipline comes to poverty and shame, but whoever heeds correction is honored."

Fill in the blanks below:

- With God's help, I will find a way to put $_____ in savings each week.

- With God's help, I will find a way to put an additional $_____ a week on my debt.

HOMEWORK

1. Make a list of additional things you could do to put something in savings each week and to pay down your debt.

2. Pray for the other members of your group and consider ways you can encourage them in their financial situation.

3. Read through next week's lesson and fill in the blanks.

4. Think of someone you know who could benefit from this course, and encourage them to sign up now for the next session.

WEEK 6: FUNDING

Opening Prayer

Welcome: Ask each member of your group to answer this question:
"If money were no object, what could you do for God?"

Scripture:

- **Read Luke 16:9** and fill in the blanks below.

  Jesus said, "I tell you, use worldly _____ to gain friends for yourselves, so that when it is gone, you will be welcomed into _____ dwellings (Heaven)."

- Jesus said we are to use the wealth God gives us (our money) to reach men, women, boys and girls with the gospel. It's not about sticks and stones, but flesh and bones.

Randy Alcorn said, "God prospers me not to raise my standard of living, but to raise my standard of giving."

God has a purpose in blessing us and giving to us – and it's not just so we can be rich.

- **Read 2 Corinthians 9:10-11** and fill in the blanks below.

  "Now He who supplies seed to the sower and bread for food will also _____ and _____ your store of seed and will enlarge the harvest of your righteousness. You will be made _____ in every way so that you can be _____ on every occasion, and through us your generosity will result in thanksgiving to God."

GOD BLESSES US SO WE CAN BE A BLESSING TO OTHERS.
Read "The Parable of the Talents" in Matthew 25:14-25 and answer the questions below:

1. In this parable, who does the master represent?

2. What do the talents represent?

3. Who do the servants represent?

4. On what basis are the servants rewarded? Does this seem fair to you?

5. How would you describe your management of the talents (financial and otherwise) God has given you? Have you developed them?

6. If the Master were to return today, in what areas of your life would He reward you for being a good steward? In what areas would He say you need to exercise more wisdom?

7. Describe one way you can use the finances God has given you to further advance His kingdom. According to this parable, what will happen to you if you use your talents to bless God's kingdom?

Jesus made it clear in **Matthew 25:27** that God wants a return on His investment. What He gives us is not just ours to keep. He wants us to develop and multiply whatever He gives us so we can accomplish even more for His purposes.

THE FOUR PURPOSES OF GOD'S BLESSING IN OUR LIVES

1. **To finance His Kingdom**

    God's plan has always been to finance the work of His Church and the spread of the Gospel of His Son, Jesus Christ, through the tithes and offerings of His people.

    Malachi 3:10, "Bring the whole tithe into the storehouse (the local church), that there may be food in my house. Test me in this," says the Lord Almighty, "and see if I will not throw open the floodgates of Heaven and pour out so much blessing that you will not have room enough for it."

    Luke 16:9, "I tell you, use worldly wealth to gain friends for yourselves, so that when it is gone, you will be welcomed into eternal dwellings."

    2 Corinthians 9:11-12, "You will be made rich in every way so that you can be generous on every occasion, and through us your generosity will result in thanksgiving to God. This service that you perform is not only supplying the needs of God's people but it is also overflowing in many expressions of thanks to God."

2. **To care for our families**

    According to **Malachi 3:10** (see above) there's a three-fold blessing that comes when we tithe.
    - #1   The needs of the church (ministry) will be met.
    - #2   Our personal needs will be met.
    - #3   God promises a surplus of blessing so we can help others.

    Philippians 4:19, "And my God will meet all your needs according to his glorious riches in Christ Jesus."

    Genesis 47:12, "Joseph also provided for his father and his brothers and all his father's household with food, according to the number of their children."

1 Timothy 5:8, "If anyone does not provide for his relatives, and especially for his immediate family, he has denied the faith and is worse than an unbeliever."

3. To meet the needs of others

God blesses us financially so we can be in a position to help others above and beyond the tithes and offerings we give to our local church.

James 2:15-17, "Suppose a brother or sister is without clothes and daily food. If one of you says to him, 'Go, I wish you well; keep warm and well fed,' but does nothing about his physical needs, what good is it? In the same way, faith by itself, if it is not accompanied by action, is dead."

Isaiah 58:10, "If you spend yourselves in behalf of the hungry and satisfy the needs of the oppressed, then your light will rise in the darkness, and your night will become like the noonday."

4. To live an abundant life

One of the best discoveries you will ever make is to learn that God wants you to use His wealth to finance His kingdom, care for our families, meet the needs of others, and enjoy an abundant life that can be handed on to future generations.

Jesus promised in **John 10:10**, "I am come that they might have life, and that they might have it more abundantly" (KJV).

1 Timothy 6:17, "Command those who are rich in this present world not to be arrogant nor to put their hope in wealth, which is so uncertain, but to put their hope in God, who richly provides us with everything for our enjoyment."

Matthew 6:33, "But seek first His (God's) kingdom and His righteousness, and all these things will be given to you as well."

Matthew 6:19-21, "Do not store up for yourselves treasures on earth, where moth and rust destroy, and where thieves break in and steal. But store up for yourselves treasures in Heaven, where moth and rust do not destroy, and where thieves do not break in and steal. For where your treasure is, there your heart will be also."

We can pass on an abundant life to future generations by modeling it and teaching it to our children.

Proverbs 13:22 says, "A good man leaves an inheritance for his children's children."

Here's one way you can make sure your children and your children's children are set for life. In fact, you could make them tax-free millionaires.

If your teenaged child or grandchild has a job, they can contribute up to $4,000 a year to a Roth IRA. The contributions aren't tax deductible, but at the child's low tax bracket, it won't matter.

All they'd have to do is put in $4,000 a year between the ages of 16 and 21, and even if they don't contribute another dime, and the Roth IRA earns 10 percent per year – they would have $2,045,042 at 65. Best of all, the money will be 100 percent tax free.*

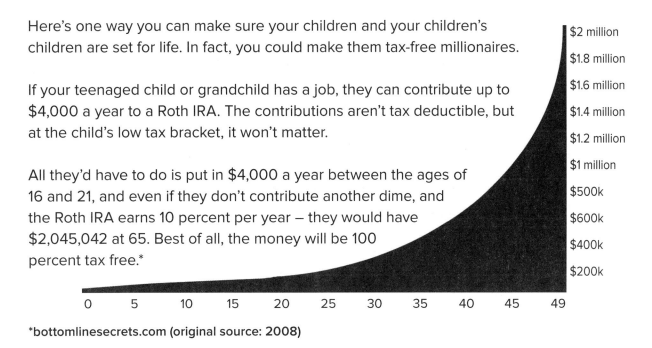

*bottomlinesecrets.com (original source: 2008)

LIST THE FOUR PURPOSES OF GOD'S BLESSINGS IN YOUR LIFE.

God blesses you financially so you can fund four primary areas:

1. To _____ His kingdom.

2. To care for our _____,

3. To _____ of others.

4. To live an _____ life.

HOMEWORK

1. Complete the worksheet on the following page that will help you determine your net worth. This is something you will want to update regularly.

2. Write out your financial goals. Now that you have a better picture of your financial situation you will be able to set specific, reachable goals.

3. Organize your financial information on your computer or print it out and place it in a folder. This would include the changes you've committed to make, your list of debts, your budget, debt payoff strategy and your net worth.

4. Keep praying for the other members of your group and their financial situations.

5. Think of someone you know who could benefit from this course and encourage them to sign up now for the next session.

YOUR PERSONAL NET WORTH

ASSETS (what you have)

Cash: $ _____

Checking Account: $ _____

Savings: $ _____

Investments: $ _____

Home: $ _____

Furnishings: $ _____

Automobiles: $ _____

Retirement/Pension: $ _____

Other: $ _____

TOTAL ASSETS: $ _____

LIABILITIES (what you owe)

Mortgage: $ _____

Automobiles: $ _____

Credit Cards: $ _____

Other Loans: $ _____

Outstanding Bills: $ _____

TOTAL LIABILITIES: $ _____

Total Assets $ _____

- Total Liabilities $ _____

YOUR NET WORTH: $ _____

DEFINITIONS

ARM

Adjustable Rate Mortgage. Your rate may fluctuate, up or down, with short-term interest indices such as the district cost of funds, corresponding treasury bills or the prime rate.

Audit

A thorough examination of your finances and accounting procedures to verify their accuracy.

Budget

A written guide for the management of your income and expenses.

Chapter 11 & 13

A legal provision which allows you to reorganize your finances and develop a repayment plan to pay off your debts.

Checkbook

A tool which allows you to write checks against the funds you have on deposit.

Compound Interest

Earning interest upon interest. This happens when interest remains in an account rather than being withdrawn.

Construction Loan

A loan which enables you to build a home or a building by paying the interest only until the loan is modified to a regular mortgage.

CPA

Certified Public Accountant

Credit Cards

Danger: avoid at all costs. These are little pieces of plastic that can get you into lots of trouble. They give you the ability to purchase things, usually at a high interest rate, which you must repay. The best way to use a credit card is to always keep a low balance and pay it off within 30 days.

Deposit

Placing money in an account at a bank or other financial institution. You should always make deposits in interest-bearing accounts whenever possible.

Dividend

A portion of earnings distributed to stockholders.

Estate Planning

A written plan to deal with the protection and transfer of your assets to others in the future.

FDIC

Federal Deposit Insurance Corporation

Interest Rate

The amount you will pay for the privilege of using someone else's money.

IRA

Individual Retirement Account

IRS

Internal Revenue Service

Late Fees

Charges you must pay for being late on your payments.

Lien

A claim enforceable by law, to have a debt or charge satisfied out of property belonging to the debtor.

Lien Release

A legal instrument to remove or discharge a judgment, mortgage or other lien as a claim against property.

Loan

An agreement where you are allowed to use someone else's money until you can pay them back the full amount. Usually with interest added.

Money Market

A savings account offered by a financial institution that pays better interest than a passbook savings account.

Mortgage

A pledge of real property as security for a debt or obligation.

Mortgage Broker

One who helps provide mortgages for consumers.

Mutual Fund

A professional stock fund that pools the money from a large number of people to gain better returns on stock investments.

NASDAQ

North Association of Securities Dealers Automated Quotation Systems

NYSE

New York Securities Exchange located in New York, NY and commonly referred to as the "big board."

PMI

Private Mortgage Insurance. If your down payment on a home is less than 20% of the appraised value or sale price, you will be required to obtain private mortgage insurance (PMI) from your lender. This protects your lender against any default on your loan.

Roth IRA

A form of IRA that allows special circumstances.

Stockbroker

One who manages stocks for shareholders.

Stocks

Money paid into a corporation by investors as common stock which becomes the permanent capital of the firm. As the corporation makes money, investors make money as well.

Tithing

The Biblical practice of giving 10% of your income to the Lord. (See Malachi 3:8-12; Matthew 23:23; Proverbs 3:9-10.)

Trusts

A legal document to preserve and protect your estate.

TSF

The Solomon Foundation, the fastest growing and now one of the largest Christian financial institutions in U.S. history based in Englewood, CO. (www.thesolomonfoundation.org)

Wall Street

Usually referred to as the financial headquarters of the world. It is located in lower Manhattan (New York, NY) and houses the NYSE and the offices of several major investment firms.

Will

A legal document to preserve and protect your assets and interests after your death. (Everyone should have one of these regardless of the size of your estate or your age.)

FREQUENTLY ASKED QUESTIONS

HOW DO YOU BALANCE A CHECKBOOK?

The simple answer is you compare all your deposits, withdrawals and all written checks with your monthly bank statement. If you have any discrepancies or questions, call your bank.

HOW DOES THE STOCK MARKET WORK?

Investors purchase stock in companies. The companies use the stock as capital to build their business. As the business grows, investors (shareholders) make money. If the businesses don't grow, investors (shareholders) lose money. This is a very volatile area and should not be attempted without professional and legal guidance.

WHEN DO I NEED TO GET A FINANCIAL PLANNER?

When you are completely out of debt and want help planning your financial future.

IF I'M IN DEBT, SHOULD I BE PUTTING MONEY IN SAVINGS OR PAY THE DEBTS OFF FIRST?

You should do both. If you have to choose, pay down your debts. Once you are debt free, you can put it all in savings.

HOW OLD DO YOU HAVE TO BE TO OPEN A CHECKING ACCOUNT?

A 16-year old can open a checking account with a parent or legal guardian as a signer. Otherwise, they have to be 18.

HOW OLD DO YOU HAVE TO BE TO OPEN AN IRA?

Anyone with earned income (and a W-2) can put up to $5,500.00 or 100% of earned income, whichever is less, in their IRA. An IRA owner who is 51 years old may also contribute an additional $1,000.00 as a catch-up contribution.

DO I NEED A CREDIT CARD TO ESTABLISH CREDIT?

It is perhaps the easiest way to establish credit. Be aware it is also one of the easiest ways to get into trouble with debt. If you use a credit card, pay it off as quickly as possible. Use it only for convenience and not as a crutch because you are undisciplined in managing your money.

HOW MUCH MONEY SHOULD I HAVE IN AN EMERGENCY FUND?

At least 3-6 months of your annual income. The more you are able to save, the better prepared you will be for emergencies.

IS IT EVER SMART TO LEASE A CAR?

If someone else is paying for it.

IS IT EVER SMART TO GET AN INTEREST-ONLY MORTGAGE?

No.

IS IT EVER SMART TO GET A REVERSE MORTGAGE?

If it is the only option available and then, only if your family and trusted Christian mentors encourage you to do so.

WHEN IS THE BEST TIME ...

1. TO PURCHASE A CAR?

*Last Tuesday or Wednesday
of the month*

Why? Dealers live for the weekend when they make most of their money.

> Fewer customers, a dealer who wants to sell cars, and a weekend off in the distance makes for better deals.

> A Monday at the end of the month is ideal, too.

2. TO PURCHASE GROCERIES?

Wednesday

You can maximize savings by combining store sales, which run from Wednesday to Tuesday. Use the latest round of coupons from your Sunday paper, too.

3. TO PURCHASE AIRLINE TICKETS?

Sunday

The common wisdom used to be Tuesday, but recent research shows the best day to buy now is on Sunday.

4. TO GO OUT TO DINNER?

Tuesday

Most restaurants start fresh on Tuesdays with fresh food. And, due to lower customer traffic, you are likely to get better service and may even get a lower price.

5. TO PURCHASE A HOTEL ROOM?

Sunday afternoon

Sunday employees are less stressed and more open to negotiation. They would rather book a room at a discount price than have an empty room.

6. TO PURCHASE GAS FOR YOUR AUTOMOBILE?

Go to GasBuddy.com and you can search your city and state, not only to find the lowest gas prices in your area, but also the best day of the week to purchase gas.

7. TO PURCHASE CLOTHING?

Thursday night

Stores are stocking their shelves for the weekend. You will find greater selections and that is also when many retailers start their weekend promotions.

8. TO PURCHASE ENTERTAINMENT TICKETS?

Show up at the box office a few hours before starting time or try stubhub.com or goldstar.com

Theaters, amusement parks and museums offer extra discounts to customers who visit mid-week. Some theaters even offer free popcorn on Wednesdays.

WORKSHEETS

LISTING OF ALL DEBTS

CREDITOR	PURCHASE	MONTHLY PAYMENT	BALANCE OWED	INTEREST RATE
TOTALS				

LISTING OF ALL DEBTS

CREDITOR	PURCHASE	MONTHLY PAYMENT	BALANCE OWED	INTEREST RATE
TOTALS				

(Additional worksheets are available online at theabcs.org/worksheets.)

G.O.O.D. FILE
(Budget)

Monthly Salary: _____

Other Income: _____

Total Income: _____

Subtract:

Tithe: _____

Taxes: _____

Monthly Spendable Income: _____

Mortgage/Rent: _____

Insurance: _____

Taxes: _____

Electric: _____

Gas: _____

Water: _____

Satellite/Cable: _____

Phone/Internet: _____

Maintenance: _____

Other: _____

Total Housing Expenses: _____

Groceries: _____

Auto Payments: _____

Gas: _____

Auto Insurance: _____

Other: _____

Total Auto Expenses: _____

Medical: _____

Life: _____

Health: _____

Total Insurance Payments: _____

Restaurants: _____

Movies/Concerts: _____

Babysitter: _____

Vacation: _____

Other: _____

Total Entertainment Expenses: _____

Clothing: _____

Dentist: _____

Doctor: _____

Prescriptions: _____

Total Medical Payments: _____

Savings: _____

Child care/school: _____

Cell phone: _____

Haircuts/nails: _____

Dry cleaning: _____

Lunches: _____

Toiletries: _____

Subscriptions: _____

Allowance/cash: _____

Holiday/Birthday Gifts: _____

Total Personal Expenses: _____

Total Expenses: _____

Monthly Spendable Income: _____

Less Total Expenses: _____

Surplus (Deficit): _____

G.O.O.D. FILE
(Budget)

Monthly Salary: _____

Other Income: _____

Total Income: _____

Subtract:

Tithe: _____

Taxes: _____

Monthly Spendable Income: _____

Mortgage/Rent: _____

Insurance: _____

Taxes: _____

Electric: _____

Gas: _____

Water: _____

Satellite/Cable: _____

Phone/Internet: _____

Maintenance: _____

Other: _____

Total Housing Expenses: _____

Groceries: _____

Auto Payments: _____

Gas: _____

Auto Insurance: _____

Other: _____

Total Auto Expenses: _____

Medical: _____

Life: _____

Health: _____

Total Insurance Payments: _____

Restaurants: _____

Movies/Concerts: _____

Babysitter: _____

Vacation: _____

Other: _____

Total Entertainment Expenses: _____

Clothing: _____

Dentist: _____

Doctor: _____

Prescriptions: _____

Total Medical Payments: _____

Savings: _____

Child care/school: _____

Cell phone: _____

Haircuts/nails: _____

Dry cleaning: _____

Lunches: _____

Toiletries: _____

Subscriptions: _____

Allowance/cash: _____

Holiday/Birthday Gifts: _____

Total Personal Expenses: _____

Total Expenses: _____

Monthly Spendable Income: _____

Less Total Expenses: _____

Surplus (Deficit): _____

(Additional worksheets are available online at theabcs.org/worksheets.)

RAPID PAYOFF STRATEGY FOR YOUR DEBTS

CREDITOR	CONTACT NUMBER	PAYOFF AMOUNT	MONTHLY PAYMENT	INTEREST RATE
TOTAL				

RAPID PAYOFF STRATEGY FOR YOUR DEBTS

CREDITOR	CONTACT NUMBER	PAYOFF AMOUNT	MONTHLY PAYMENT	INTEREST RATE
TOTAL				

(Additional worksheets are available online at theabcs.org/worksheets.)

YOUR PERSONAL NET WORTH

ASSETS (what you have)

Cash:	$ _____
Checking Account:	$ _____
Savings:	$ _____
Investments:	$ _____
Home:	$ _____
Furnishings:	$ _____
Automobiles:	$ _____
Retirement/Pension:	$ _____
Other:	$ _____
TOTAL ASSETS:	$ _____

LIABILITIES (what you owe)

Mortgage:	$ _____
Automobiles:	$ _____
Credit Cards:	$ _____
Other Loans:	$ _____
Outstanding Bills:	$ _____
TOTAL LIABILITIES:	$ _____

Total Assets	$ _____
- Total Liabilities	$ _____

YOUR NET WORTH: $ _____

YOUR PERSONAL NET WORTH

ASSETS (what you have)

Cash: $ _____

Checking Account: $ _____

Savings: $ _____

Investments: $ _____

Home: $ _____

Furnishings: $ _____

Automobiles: $ _____

Retirement/Pension: $ _____

Other: $ _____

TOTAL ASSETS: $ _____

LIABILITIES (what you owe)

Mortgage: $ _____

Automobiles: $ _____

Credit Cards: $ _____

Other Loans: $ _____

Outstanding Bills: $ _____

TOTAL LIABILITIES: $ _____

Total Assets $ _____

- Total Liabilities $ _____

YOUR NET WORTH: $ _____

(Additional worksheets are available online at theabcs.org/worksheets.)

ANSWER KEY

WEEK 1

n/a

WEEK 2

servant
love

WEEK 3

obey
sacrifice
wealth
firstfruits
filled
first
things
given
the Lord
Tithing
choose
master
the Lord
Tithing

WEEK 4

right
death
Lord
own
straight

WEEK 5

encouragement
encourage
build
He
I
Tithing
grow
servant

WEEK 6

wealth
eternal
supply
increase
rich
generous
finance
families
meet the needs
abundant

The New ABCs of Financial Freedom, by Barry L. Cameron, is radically changing how churches, individuals and families view God's instruction conerning money, debt, budgets and stewardship. *The New ABCs of Financial Freedom* was written to help people discover God's way for managing the resources He entrusts to us. *The New ABCs of Financial Freedom* is also available in Spanish.

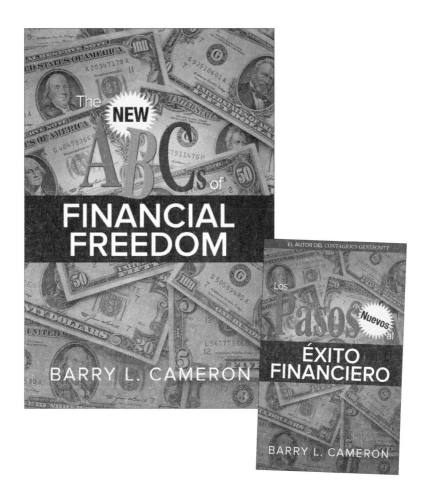

Order your copy today at 1.888.360.7648, by email at info@thediscipleshop.com or at thediscipleshop.com.

FOR ADDITIONAL HELP WITH YOUR FINANCES:

Generosity is always contagious!
It's also supposed to be our normal way of life.

*"If you were blessed by Barry's book, The ABCs of Financial Freedom,
you'll be blessed even more by Contagious Generosity."*

*"Wow! What a great book! Barry Cameron has given us, in Contagious Generosity,
a clarion call to discover the joy and fulfillment of becoming and
being God's agents of blessing to others."*

*"Get ready to be surprised, challenged, and inspired. Practicing these principles will not
only change your life, but change our world for the better."*

*"Barry Cameron practices what he preaches. I have watched Barry and the congregation
he serves live out their commitment to contagious generosity."*

Order your copy today at 1.888.360.7648, by email at
info@thediscipleshop.com or at thediscipleshop.com.

TO CONTACT THE AUTHOR:

Barry L. Cameron, Senior Pastor
Crossroads Christian Church
6450 South Highway 360
Grand Prairie, TX 75052

(817) 557-2277
pastorcameron@crossroadschristian.org
crossroadschristian.org

For more resources by Barry L. Cameron, contact:
info@thediscipleshop.com
or 1.888.360.7648

FOLLOW BARRY CAMERON ON
/BarryLCameron
@BarryLCameron
@BarryLCameron
linkedin.com/pub/barry-cameron/32/538/6aa